More praise for *Jacob's Journey*

ALSO BY NOAH benShea

Jacob the Baker

Jacob's
Journey

Jacob's Journey

WISDOM TO FIND THE WAY,

STRENGTH TO CARRY ON

Noah benShea

Ballantine Books
New York

Library of Congress Catalog Card Number: 92-90045

ISBN: 0-345-37799-0

Cover design by Kristine V. Mills
Cover art by Stephen Alcorn

Manufactured in the United States of America
First Ballantine Books Edition: November 1992
10 9 8 7 6 5 4 3 2 1

*To the quiet heroism of those
who carry on*

. . . *Jacob instead turned inside, swam through a familiar sea to an island in himself, to a time when his island had been ignored, to a time when others would pay no attention to a baker who bent over his workbench, writing notes to himself while the day was still dark.*

Then, all of this had changed. Changed when one of Jacob's notes had found its way into a loaf of bread. Changed because, when the note was discovered, Jacob's anonymity was lost forever.

Caught in the downpour of this attention, the question now was whether the twists in Jacob's life would cause his garden to flood, while those around him gave thanks for rain. . . .

—Jacob's Journey

*I am sending an angel in front of
you to guard you as you go
and to guide you to the place
I have prepared.*
                    —Exodus 23:20

Thank You
to Danyel benShea
for being the remarkable person she is
and to all of those who have extended
their hand along the way.

Contents

Contents

Contents

Contents

Contents

Contents

Jacob's Journey

HOPE FOR THE BEST;
MAKE PEACE
WITH THE REST

*J*acob woke but did not open his eyes. Moving from sleep to prayer, he made the world whole again, found his place, and gave thanks.

The day before dawn was still dark, colored by the night's black certainty. When Jacob opened his eyes and looked around the small room, he prayed that time would also diminish the shadows cast by his own ignorance.

As the soles of his feet settled on the wooden floor, the cold jarred him, reminding him of sliding from his bed as a boy, and urged him to dress quickly in front of the small heater.

A loaf of dark bread sat on the scarred edge of the narrow table where Jacob ate. Using his thumb and forefinger, he pulled at the soft center of the bread until it gave way.

He sipped at his breakfast tea while clenching a cube of sugar between his teeth. When the tea melted caves in the sugar, Jacob wondered if he weren't drinking from a well in the Garden of Eden.

He ate his meal slowly and deliberately. He undid his moments with patience, treating his time as a gift, and luxuriated not in his possessions but in his pace.

A book he had been reading the night before remained open next to Jacob. His awareness fell on the white curve of the book's fanning pages. In their flutter he saw the wings of a dove and the prayer that a man named Noah might have sent forth, hoping faith would offer his soul sanctuary in a storm.

Jacob took a breath and released it, remembering the quiet before the flood of attention had risen around him in the past year, and wondered if his *own* ark would hold.

He lifted himself slowly from his chair and looked down to see if perhaps a weight did not sit on his lap. He pushed the grains of bread from the table into the palm of his hand and then dropped them into the pocket of his jacket. It was time to leave for the bakery.

Jacob wrapped a thick scarf around his collar, crossed the ends under his chin, and opened the front door. He did not paint the day with his experience of the day before nor measure his appreciation for being alive by his anticipation of what the day would bring.

A charcoal sky hung in front of Jacob like a black canopy tacked to the heavens. Jacob wondered if the silver stars might not have been pasted against the black as the planet's reward for good behavior.

As he stepped across the threshold, an arm reached out and took Jacob by the elbow, connecting him to a pale young man whose mouth worked nervously even before he spoke.

"Jacob, I'm sorry," began the voice with apology. "I'm sorry to bother you so early, but others in the community told me that this is a time when there are not so many people asking you questions."

"If you did not disturb me, I'd be forced to disturb myself," said Jacob.

The wind whipped around Jacob's legs and cut at the back of his knees. While signaling the boy to keep up with him, Jacob began walking at a pace that soon caused the distance between them to widen.

The world held white and silent in the night's new snow, unbroken in its sleep. Jacob glided on the quiet.

When he paused to look for the boy behind him, Jacob saw the footprints his own boots left in the snow. He knew that within hours the sun would erase any trace of this journey, and he smiled, amused by his insignificance.

"Jacob," called the boy, his voice trailing, "I am young and unsure of myself. How should I live my life?"

"Hope for the best and make peace with the rest," said Jacob without slowing.

"But," said the boy, who found himself almost running to stay in stride, "what should I *do* with my life?"

Jacob stopped and reached out as if to touch a thought he had laid on a shelf. "Be yourself. Do that. And now, if you will excuse me, I must be a baker."

Jacob moved down the dark streets and past the collage of homes. The faces of those who had come and gone appeared and disappeared behind windows curtained by a veil of ice. What time takes, memory replaces, thought Jacob. He hurried on.

Soon Jacob turned a corner he had turned many times in his life and found himself facing the back of the bakery. The brick walls on both sides pressed together, appearing almost to touch as they grew taller. A line of pigeons trailed one another in a figure eight, each poking the ground for a crumb of bread the bird before it might have missed.

At Jacob's arrival, the pigeons, frantic with excitement, rose and hovered beneath the rain gutters. Beating their wings, they made the music of muffled applause. Jacob thought of King Solomon, who spoke the language of birds.

When the pigeons settled, some of them came to rest on Jacob's shoulders, seeking the crumbs he pulled from his pocket.

Although once only the birds had been here to greet Jacob with their hunger and cold, this morning a form covered by a cape of snow also waited, wearily marching in place and stamping its feet to fight the cold.

The figure turned toward Jacob, presenting the face of an old man.

"I had no place to go."

"Where are any of us going?" answered Jacob, moving, along with the figure, up the stairs of the loading dock.

"I have traveled far to see you," said the voice, with persistence.

"Time turns every destination into a point of departure," said Jacob, shifting his foot from the top step to the landing.

The key to the bakery's back door felt cold, and stuck to Jacob's hand as it turned slowly in the lock.

Reassuring himself that faith was more than entering a familiar blindness boldly, Jacob stepped into the bakery, left the dark before dawn for the greater darkness of the empty building.

Jacob knelt to check the pilot light before firing the large oven. The flame still flickered. He paused and gave thanks that it had remained through the night, and prayed that he, too, had not forgotten how to conduct himself.

Soon the oven gained temperature, and Jacob, putting his hands on the old man's shoulders, drew him over so he might rest against the bricks of the warming walls.

Then, returning his attention to the bakery, Jacob began to empty flour into the huge mixer. As the flour collected on itself, it made mountains—mountains that in moments slid down the sides of the bowl.

The snow that rested on the old man began to melt. He looked down with confusion into the pool forming at his feet. "Do you know who I am?" he asked.

"You are someone who was cold," said Jacob, without judgment. He began adding water to the mixer and watched as the water disappeared beneath the flour, running like life's secrets just below the surface.

"Do you want something from me?" asked the old man, his voice curving with suspicion.

Jacob felt the mixer's arm shudder before it turned to its tireless cycle.

"I want you not to be cold," said Jacob, careful now not to dress his caring in pity.

The old man said nothing, yet his perplexity remained, hanging over him like a halo.

Jacob took the fresh dough from the mixer, and as he began to work it into loaves, he looked again at the stranger and wondered how it was that all of us, created from the same Hand and the same clay, became such different vessels.

"What will the others say when they discover that you have taken a man like *me* into the bakery?" asked the stranger.

"What would they have said about *me* if I had not taken you in?" said Jacob.

"But I am not your responsibility," said the man.

"Perhaps you are right," said Jacob, smiling, "but how I conduct myself *is* my responsibility."

The stranger returned Jacob's smile, his fears fading.

Jacob touched the tip of his finger to the rising loaves, watched the surface collapse, and waited for the loaves to rise again before slipping them onto the shelves of the oven.

As the pans journeyed on their endless wheel, the stranger asked, "When will the bread be ready?"

"Patience is the shortest route on a long journey," answered Jacob.

"And how did *you* find your way to this wisdom?" asked the stranger.

Jacob waved off the question, embarrassed by the vanity of accepting it.

"Then tell me what wisdom teaches us," asked the stranger.

Jacob answered with a distracted conviction. "It is wiser to be kind than to be wise," he said, as if this were a matter he had settled long ago.

The man thought about Jacob's words and then said, "I will never forget you, Jacob."

"Too often we remember what would be wise to forget," said Jacob.

Jacob lifted a loaf of bread from the oven. The heat was still venting from the bread's crust. He offered it to the stranger.

The man hesitated, unsure what to do. Then he wrapped both arms around the warm loaf and pulled it to his chest, drawing from the warmth.

Jacob again turned to his work. He lifted a sack of flour and felt lighter as the weight of the flour, rather than the stranger's compliments, fell across his back.

The stranger moved haltingly to leave. He stopped once more by the door to look at Jacob, then began his way down the stairs, slipping almost invisibly past the line of men who were now arriving for work.

The doors to the day were thrown open. Morning painted the room with light. Clouds of flour dust rolled a white carpet across the floor.

The bakery now became a hive of hands braiding loaves and tying rolls. Sheets of cake were cut and layered. Circles of cookie dough were dropped into set patterns on broad pans.

While those around him worked, Jacob served as their point of balance. In his rhythm was their pace. He did not seek to exercise this influence, and yet the others, like diverse ingredients unaware of a higher purpose, were somehow drawn into Jacob's recipe until, out of many, grew one. For Jacob, the joy of this experience was in being part of something larger than himself. In this way he touched the notion of family and experienced the embrace that someone who lives alone might not have known.

Max, the young man who lifted the heavy pallets and trays, let the doors close loudly behind him.

"Hey, Jacob! Who was that guy I saw leaving earlier?"

"A teacher," answered Jacob.

"*That* old man?" asked Max.

"Those from whom we do not learn reflect only our *own* ignorance," said Jacob.

"Oh yeah?" added Max. "Well, we don't need another teacher. We have you."

"I am a baker," said Jacob.

"Anything you say," said Max. "But to the people already waiting outside to talk to you, you're their *tzadik*, their holy man."

Although he could hear what Max was saying, Jacob didn't answer. He watched instead as the mixer's arm lifted and fell, folded and refolded the dough.

Although Max's voice strained to touch Jacob with its flattery, Jacob instead turned inside, swam through a familiar sea to an island in himself, to a time when his island had been ignored, to a time when others would pay no attention to a baker who bent over his workbench, writing notes to himself while the day was still dark.

Then, all of this had changed. Changed when one of Jacob's notes had found its way into a loaf of bread. Changed because, when the note was discovered, Jacob's anonymity was lost forever.

Caught in the downpour of this attention, the question now was whether the twists in Jacob's life would cause his garden to flood, while those around him gave thanks for rain.

As Max had warned, a crowd soon gathered around Jacob. They waited like an impatient aura, preparing to make him more than a baker, and anxious to crown him with their dilemmas.

When Jacob looked up, everyone around him began to talk at once. The questions advanced like infantry, and although Jacob stood his ground, he watched his world retreat. Although he knew his lines intuitively, he was no longer sure he recognized the role that he was now asked to perform.

Ever since the community had discovered Jacob's wisdom in their bread, he always submitted to their requests and pleas. Still, it was as a baker that Jacob knew himself, and it was left to Samuel, the owner of the bakery, to scale the demands that weighed on Jacob.

"All right, all right," said Samuel, pulling at the outer circle of the crowd and shouting more out of habit than anger. "Give the man some room. Let him do his job. The sages say, 'Without bread there is no wisdom.' Isn't that right, Jacob?"

Jacob said nothing, hearing this as Samuel's caring for him masked as a question.

Somehow, a child had squeezed through the legs of those who had been standing in front of her. She tugged at Jacob's pants, and found a friend when their faces met.

"Jacob," said the little girl, "my parents say I ask too many questions."

"All experience begins with wonder," said Jacob.

"But my parents don't understand me," said the girl.

"Be understanding of them," said Jacob, "and be thankful. Some parents love knowing. Others know love."

The child turned quiet and then disappeared amid the forest of legs that had again sprung up around her.

An elderly woman raised her voice.

"Jacob, I'm afraid of growing old."

" 'Growing old' is a contradiction in terms," said Jacob.

"What about me?" asked a voice filled with humility. "Where should I look for learning? I am only a common man."

"Turn inward," said Jacob, "and you will find the wisdom of common sense."

"And, now, now you will let the baker bake!" said Samuel, shooing people toward the back door as if they were pigeons that had pecked long enough at Jacob's grains of truth.

The surrounding faces dissolved. Jacob was again alone with his work. He could hear the sounds of palms patting dough and smell the different breads baking. He placed the flat of his cheek on the side of the old oven, like a boy might lay his head on his father's chest.

There is only work and love in life, thought Jacob. If we are fortunate, we love our work. If we are wise, we are willing to work at love.

On the way home, at the end of the day, Jacob walked past fields with large bales of hay rolled and covered for the winter. He thought of his friend Mr. Gold, who was gone, and decided to visit his grave.

At the foot of the grave, tiny streams of melting snow ran like veins in the grass and formed a pattern at Jacob's feet. When Jacob moved his fingers across the granite marker, he could feel in its rough cracks the way time fractured friendship. The cold snapped at him, and he turned toward home.

That evening, Jacob ate his meal in what was now the rare solitude of his books and his thoughts.

While he ate, his mind wandered and, like a wanderer who carries all of his clothes by wearing them, Jacob began to peel away the layers of himself until he came to the naked center, where his perspective was not a point of view. There, too, like a traveler, he pressed his nose curiously against his own window.

In the intimacy of this moment, marked by neither time nor space, Jacob took his flat baker's pencil from his back pocket and found himself not so much writing as taking notes, not so much using words to sketch a scene as employing language to trace a landscape from within.

Soon, pieces of paper scratched with his thoughts surrounded him like confetti. It was as if the heavens had opened and showered Jacob, thrown a party to remind him of what he already knew. "We are all lost," said the slip resting next to Jacob's teacup, "and our only hope of being found is in knowing this."

The next morning, when Jacob walked to the bakery, his experience was not the effort of lifting his feet but of keeping his balance while a great wheel rolled under him.

In the half-light of the bakery, Jacob spread cornmeal on the bread boards, preparing them for the men who would arrive after him. As he stacked one board on top of another, Jacob noticed that the fingerprint of his thumb left its swirls in the dust. It is like signing my name in the sand, thought Jacob. I am here until the tides.

The room warmed as waves of heat shimmered in front of the ovens. Jacob looked around him, sensed an isolated calm, and floated in the moment, knowing that, for a man to dream, he must be prepared to put his self to rest.

Now, however, there was little rest for Jacob. More and more often, people from the community came and edged their bodies into the space around him. They asked Jacob to find doors in their dilemmas while he strained to lift trays of bread from the oven. They poured out their hearts while he emptied a sack of flour into the mixer. They pleaded with him for simple solutions while he labored at kneading the dough. And while his neighbors spoke, Jacob listened and smiled and wondered if others did not think he sometimes looked more tired than wise.

Still, Jacob always answered his neighbors in the manner of a gentle friend—a friend prepared to sit with them through the night, a friend who somehow understands that what often passes for everyday living is in fact heroic; that what often passes for heroism is in fact faith; that what often passes for faith is in fact hope.

Jacob gave of his wisdom as if he were a porter helping others set down their baggage. In this way, his neighbors did not feel that their questions were a weight to Jacob but a lessening of their own lading. When they told Jacob that he had a great gift, he would shield his eyes as if their compliment were blinding. *"Life* is a gift," said Jacob. "Open yours."

This morning, Samuel's voice cut through the bakery, shouting, "Jacob! Jacob!" with a tone of insistence that arrived before the owner could skirt the racks and tables that crowded his bakery.

Following in Samuel's hurry, and magnetized like a collective shadow to his excitement, were a flock of faces from the community. All appeared to be out of breath, their eyes bulging. Jacob looked up from his work. His calm rode out to meet Samuel's rush. Then Samuel held up his arms, and the parade behind him came to a halt.

Samuel did his best to cover his energy and subdue himself before speaking. Nevertheless, when he began, he was like a pot bubbling on the verge of boiling.

"Jacob," asked Samuel, as if they were alone, "how are you?"

Samuel asked the question much like a friend might knock on another friend's door as a courtesy before entering. Jacob's smile answered the door without answering the question.

Samuel draped his arm around Jacob's shoulder in an act of intimacy, which also sheltered their conversation.

"Listen, Jacob," began Samuel. "A delegation has arrived from our village. They want to talk with you."

As Samuel spoke, he tried to read Jacob's reaction in his eyes. Jacob, however, shut his eyes and simply listened.

"They say," continued Samuel, now a bit nervous, "that they *must* speak with you."

Again Samuel searched for some sign from Jacob, the feelings behind his features. But Jacob's emotions had left no trail.

"Well?" said Samuel, hoping for Jacob's consideration.

Silence.

"Well?" said Samuel again, this time wringing his hands.

Again silence. And then, "What would you like me to do?" asked Jacob, implying his consent in a voice so faint it was almost lost in the bakery.

"Thank you, thank you, Jacob," said Samuel, beside himself with appreciation. "These people do all of us great honor by coming here."

Those who entered the bakery with Samuel now swelled behind Jacob. They swept him forward past the old oven, around the bakery boards covered with cornmeal, and through the swinging doors.

Once, Jacob had taught the children who came to learn from him that a fish could not describe water until it had been caught; could not know its element until it had been removed from its constant. Now Jacob felt the bite in the barb of this awareness, felt pulled by a distant line into the retail section of the bakery, into this public otherworld, and felt some part of his soul begin to fight for air.

Although the room Jacob entered was crowded with conversation, Samuel's momentum carried them forward. When Samuel stopped, the wave of people behind Jacob fell away. Standing in front of Jacob, and across a narrow gulf of floor that was now suddenly empty, were two men and a woman.

"Here he is!" said Samuel, almost bowing.

The woman, responding to a nod from the man on her right, stepped forward.

"Are you Jacob?" the woman asked, as if inquiring about the ground rules of a game yet to be played.

Jacob answered, "Yes," wondering if he was confessing to more than she asked.

"Jacob," said the woman, repeating his name as a way of confirming her stance, "people say you are a *tzadik*, a holy man. Is this true?"

"All work is holy," said Jacob. "I am a baker."

The woman smiled and turned back to her companions so that they might confer.

Now the man on the left looked to Jacob. He began to speak with the guile of a hunter laying a trap. "Jacob, we have been told that you said it is wiser to be kind than to be wise. But," asked the man, now ready to spring his trap, "is it wise to love without reason?"

"The world," said Jacob, "was not created as an act of reason but as an act of love. And the reason for love is not reason."

A murmur of what the man had asked and what Jacob had answered hovered like clouds of dialogue over the crowd.

Finally, the last of the delegation took his place.

"Jacob," began the man, "you have said that the love we give is never taken from us, and yet all of us in this community have taken a great deal from you."

The tone in the man's voice spoke of Jacob as if he were a treasure whose value had at last been accurately appraised and established.

Jacob said nothing. His eyes welled with self-consciousness.

Then came the man's announcement. "Jacob, we seek to honor you. From now on you no longer need to be a baker! The community has decided that we will support you as you have been such a source of strength to us."

The hook was set. Jacob saw himself gasping on the shore. He looked at Samuel with disbelief, but Samuel, smiling and rubbing his ample belly proudly, was part of the community.

Without warning, everyone rushed forward. They engulfed Jacob in a sea of arms and congratulations, whispered in waves that he deserved this honor, told him in tides that nothing like this had ever happened before, washed over him with offers of food and clothing.

The community had not waited for Jacob's answer. They used his silence as consent, inflating *themselves* with the buoyancy of the moment. Jacob did not feel so much honored as ignored.

Then those who urged and smiled and touched Jacob were gone, leaving the bakery with the delegation, assuring themselves that they had done the right thing.

Jacob again stood alone. He drifted into the deserted bakery, stared at the stack of bread boards, and wondered at how the print he had left in the cornmeal had smeared under pressure from above and below. To control ourselves, thought Jacob, we must realize *we* are not in control.

Samuel returned to the bakery by himself. There he found Jacob rocking back and forth in prayer on the creaking wooden floor. After the community's offer, Samuel wondered what more Jacob could be praying for. Then Samuel looked around the bakery and found himself unexpectedly haunted by a fear that Jacob's trust had slipped between his fingers like time.

"Jacob," said Samuel tentatively, hesitant to begin, hesitant not to begin, "have we done harm by rewarding you in this way?"

"No," said Jacob, turning to meet his friend's concern, "but I cannot accept."

"But you *must*," said Samuel, his eagerness edged with demand. "It is impossible for you to remain in the bakery. *You* can't get any work done. *We* can't get any work done. There are too many people who want to see you." Samuel paused. "There are too many who *need* to see you," he added, correcting himself and hoping what he described as Jacob's responsibility would moderate a nagging doubt he had of his *own* accountability.

While Samuel spoke, Jacob listened. While he listened, Jacob imagined he saw a road appearing from the woods behind his home. He wondered if he took this road, where it would lead. He wondered if he *was* a *tzadik*, who would be his, wondered if any teacher was wise enough to be his own student.

"You know, Samuel," said Jacob, reconciling his route to reality, "our path in life is often not our decision but how we decide to live with decisions that have already been made."

Jacob looked down at the flour dust at his feet, saw in the dust a harbinger of the road ahead, knew some part of him had already begun his journey.

"I am Jacob the baker," said Jacob to Samuel, as if meeting him for the first time. "I am honored to be thought of as more, but if I cannot be what I am, then I cannot be where I am. It is time for me to go."

"What do you mean?" asked Samuel.

"I mean a man must be at home with himself," said Jacob.

"Jacob," said Samuel, who saw himself losing not only a teacher but a friend, "where will you find an oven to warm your cheek? Where will you find a baker's bench to scribble your thoughts? Where will you find children like those who sat on the flour sacks and laughed and learned with you?"

"Yes," answered Jacob. "Where, Samuel, if not here?"

Samuel had not thought this could happen. He could not raise an argument. He could speak only from loss.

"We will miss you," said Samuel.

Jacob looked at his friend and then spoke in a voice that was more prayer than answer.

"Though our mind knows a path, our heart is the way. If you miss me, then draw near to me by loving God. And draw near to God . . . by loving those around you."

BECAUSE EACH OF US IS
ALONE ON OUR JOURNEY,
WE SOMETIMES PACK
OUR FEARS FOR COMPANY

*T*he morning Jacob began his journey, he rose and wrapped himself in his prayer shawl. Then he folded his prayers and dressed as if he were leaving for the bakery.

He packed to take with him only the bread and clothing that would fit in a small canvas bag.

Before closing the door behind him, Jacob stopped and turned. He looked back into his empty rooms as if to check that his eyes saw what he already knew he was carrying in his heart.

Almost immediately, a young woman who stood outside his house rushed up to him. "Jacob, if you leave, who will be here to teach us?"

And Jacob answered, "Wisdom surrounds us. It is seldom hidden but often overlooked. When we shut our eyes, the truth does not go into hiding."

FEAR BEGINS
....
BEFORE *WE* BEGIN

*I*n the books of wisdom Jacob had studied as a boy, it was said that every time a door shut, somewhere another door opened. Now, feeling not so much pushed as pulled, Jacob walked through the day, watching it move from dark to light to shades of gray. Behind him the distant outline of his village lost form and then flattened. *What* was dissolved into *what would be.*

That evening, on the verge of a great forest, features carved by time looked out at Jacob from the trunks of the surrounding trees. Jacob stopped and stood beside the largest of the trees, hearing the tree's limbs moaning as they shifted in the wind, hearing his own prayers in their groaning.

Ahead of him, Jacob saw a woman's silhouette, and like the dark green boughs that hung over her, the woman's shoulders seemed to sag under her shawl.

Jacob's pace soon brought him even with the woman. When he came up next to her, he tossed his welcome as if it were pebbles thrown against a shuttered window.

The woman raised her head and discovered Jacob's smile. Then her sadness moved to confusion. His warmth was a garment she had been handed but had no place to hang.

Jacob sensed the woman's bewilderment and watched her insecurity mature to doubt. To calm her, Jacob offered the woman not his strength but his vulnerability. He explained that he was a stranger and did not know the path, and asked if she would walk with him, show *him* the way.

"Why do you ask *me* for help?" she complained, laboring to lift herself from the depth of her spirit. "Can't you see I am an old woman who is alone?"

"Each of us is alone," said Jacob. "And because each of us is alone on our journey, we sometimes pack our fears for company."

The old woman looked at Jacob. "You may be right," she said, and then, laughing to herself, "but sometimes our fears can keep us warm."

"And sometimes," said Jacob, "we are afraid of losing the fears that keep us warm."

"Well . . ." said the woman, unsure, cautious of touching her courage.

Jacob looked over his shoulder and saw the moon, full and silver, suspended against the night, knew that somewhere beneath the moon was where he had begun the day.

"Fear," said Jacob, turning back to the woman, "fear makes us not only less than we might be but less than we think we are. Faith reminds us we should doubt our fears."

Jacob motioned to the path ahead of them. "Perhaps we can lean on each other for a while."

The woman laughed out loud. "How can I be a support to you?"

"Ah, that is not so difficult," said Jacob. "You see, the difference between a Tower of Babel and a tower of strength is the difference between those who live to make themselves more and those who know the way to heaven is in making others more."

ANY MOMENT
GROWS LOUDER
WHEN SURROUNDED
BY SILENCE

Jacob and the old woman traveled on together through the night, talked of their lives, diminished the darkness by sharing it, and watched the stars rise and fall toward morning.

"Jacob," the woman asked, pulling her shawl tighter around her, "are you lonely being so far from home?"

"A man who is alone with himself is not without company," said Jacob.

"Yes, but do you miss the people who would come to see you each day?"

"My own questions visited me," said Jacob, "long before others knocked on my door."

"Certainly," said the old woman, placing one foot slowly after the other, "you must have gotten tired of your own questions?"

"Actually," said Jacob, turning to look for a moment at the path behind him, "it was my answers that I found most tiresome."

"So," asked the woman, pointing to Jacob's satchel and to the road that now turned in two directions, "before I leave you, tell me, have you brought your questions with you on this journey?"

Jacob lifted his shoulders, shrugging with an air of helplessness. "What else could I do with my questions?" he asked. "I have never discovered how to unpack them. What I do not know always travels with me. And, after all, when we begin a journey, are any of us capable of leaving our ignorance at home?"

A FOOL IS SOMEONE
WHO KNOWS TOO MUCH
TO LEARN ANYTHING

When Jacob turned over, he could feel the sun on his face. He saw morning as a triangle of blue sky framed in the limbs of a large oak. The tree that had taken Jacob into its curve during the night still stood guard over him.

A voice called out, "Are you Jacob the baker?" The voice cut like an ax, and Jacob fell from the forever back into the now.

Jacob was unsure what was expected of him. He said nothing.

"I was told I could find you on this path," the voice persisted.

Directly opposite him, Jacob saw a man whose eyes searched others as if rummaging drawers for gold coins.

"Let me ask you a question," said the man, fueled by his own encouragement. "Why is it that, even though I am rich, my life feels empty?"

"Some people have nothing because they have the courage to reach out and take it," said Jacob.

The man, less sure of himself, looked at Jacob with suspicion. "Well, when others turn to me for help because I am rich, what should I say?"

"Say thank you," said Jacob, fingering the edges of a leaf that had fallen from the canopy of the oak.

"What?" said the man. "Why should I say thank you?" His voice again grew louder as if to boost his confidence. "What can the poor give me?"

"Have you ever met a man whose success is not also a burden?" said Jacob. "Charity allows you to lessen your load. In this way, having less can add to your life."

Now the stranger took a new tone. "I feel like a fool," he said.

"A fool is someone who knows too much to learn anything," said Jacob.

"I don't understand," said the man.

"Good," said Jacob, turning once again to the path before him. "Only a man who is not filled with himself can be increased by others."

TAKING
A MOMENT
EXPANDS TIME

*J*acob watched one foot rise and fall, only to be replaced by the other. The journey of days had become weeks. And Jacob wondered what would become of him.

From the beginning, he knew not so much *where* he was going but that it had been time for him to leave. If every moment was holy, thought Jacob, then every step that has brought me here is sacred. That others in his community did not understand his leaving did not disturb him. Reason, after all, would travel only so far; it made no sense for it to go any farther.

Jacob looked down at his path as if it were the current of a great river. As he stared into the flow, he saw the seemingly unending line of moments given to him. Then, like a man marking a trail, he began to put his prayers between the moments, making the common profound by pausing.

Using prayer to tie knots in time, Jacob isolated the details that would pass before others as a stream of events.

In this way Jacob secured the moments in his life, returned their individuality, allowed the luster in each of them to be observed, and appreciated and saved, transformed his moments into a string of pearls.

THOSE WHO KNOW
EVERYTHING
USUALLY KNOW LESS

*T*he trail now took Jacob up a winding ridge of foothills, alternately exposing him to bitter cold and heat. From the summit, Jacob looked down on his path and reminded himself that the shortest distance between two points is knowing that we spend most of our life going in circles.

He sat to rest on a large rock, which ice and rain had sculpted into a chair. He watched birds soaring on thermal currents and felt the invisible Hand that had lifted him from all that was familiar and held him suspended so far from home.

At evening, Jacob came upon a small house protected from the wind on three sides by the slope of the land around it. Outside of the house, the man who lived there gathered wood for the night's fire.

"You had a long climb up this mountain," said the man.

"Yes," said Jacob, wiping his brow, "but even Moses had to climb a mountain."

"And what did Moses learn from climbing his mountain?" asked the man, amused by the conversation and the company.

"Moses," said Jacob, "like the rest of us, discovered that to come down the mountain and live with your vision takes as much effort as climbing the mountain in pursuit of your vision."

The man smiled at Jacob's answer and invited him into his home, offering him dinner and a place to spend the night.

The man's wife, also pleased with the prospect of company, prepared a place for Jacob next to the fire, where he could share in its reflected warmth. The couple's two children came and sat across from Jacob. As the light from the fire danced in their eyes, Jacob wondered how it was that we ever allowed such a flame to become extinguished.

After dinner, the children turned to Jacob and asked if he would tell them a story. "A story about what?" asked Jacob.

"About a giant," squealed the children.

Jacob smiled, leaned against the warm stones at the side of the fireplace, and began, his voice turning softly inward.

"Once there was a boy who asked his father to take him to see the great parade that passed through the village where they lived. The father, remembering the parade from when he was a boy, quickly agreed, and the next morning the boy and his father set out together.

"As they approached the route the parade would take, people started to push in from all sides, and the crowd grew thick. When the people along the way became almost a wall, the father lifted his son and placed him on his shoulders, as his own father had once done for him.

"Soon the parade began, and as it passed, the boy kept telling his father how wonderful it was, how spectacular were the colors and images. The boy, in fact, grew so prideful of what he saw that he mocked those who saw less, saying even to his father, 'If only you could see what I see.'

"But," said Jacob, staring straight into the faces of the children, "what the boy did not look at was *why* he could see. What the boy forgot was that once his father, too, could see."

Then, as if he had finished the story, Jacob stopped speaking and simply looked at the fire. The children turned to Jacob, showing disappointment at how the story had ended.

"Is that it?" said the girl. "We thought you were going to tell us a story about a giant."

"But I did," said Jacob, smiling, watching how silence invited expectation. "I told you a story about a boy who *could* have been a giant."

"How?" squealed the children.

"A giant," said Jacob, "is anyone who remembers we are all sitting on someone else's shoulders."

"And what does it make us if we don't remember?" asked the boy.

"A burden," answered Jacob.

"What if *I* get on my brother's shoulders?" asked the girl, giggling.

"Ah," said Jacob, smiling back at the girl, "although anyone is small who is unable to see past their own opinions, giants can also be small people cooperating."

The room had grown warm. The windows fogged. Soon the family fell asleep, and the cat curled near the heels of the father's work boots.

Observing the simple truths that surrounded him, Jacob took his baker's pencil from his canvas bag and wrote a note to himself: "The way to discover what is of value in life is by taking the time to treasure the moments."

Jacob buried the note in the bottom of his bag and placed the bag under his head for a pillow. The smell of smoke from the fire clung to Jacob's beard. Shaking the front door, the wind felt the hinges for their strength.

AN OPEN MIND IS A PATH
TO AN OPEN HEART

*T*he woman woke in the morning and found Jacob finishing his prayers. She offered him coffee and asked if she might speak with him. Jacob put the coffee cup on the chair next to the bed and thought of the cup of tea he drank when *his* house was his home.

"You seem like someone I can talk to," said the woman, hoping Jacob would agree with her estimation.

Jacob invited the woman in by opening his heart.

"Jacob," the woman began, challenging her doubts by speaking quickly, "when I try to talk with my husband, he tells me to leave him alone. And when I leave him alone, he tells me I'm not giving him any attention. What should I do?"

"Perhaps you have to decide whether you are looking for love or searching for reason," said Jacob.

"I don't understand," said the woman.

"Understanding love is different than being in love," said Jacob. "Love is not only an affair of the mind."

"Well," said the woman, "my husband and I need a miracle."

"A miracle," said Jacob, "is our capacity to bury hate and grow love."

"But our love is tired," said the woman. "We've grown weary of each other."

"We usually fall asleep in our relationships," said Jacob, "not because we are tired of love but so we can dream of new relationships. Life, however, is a work in progress, and love's challenge, over time, is not to see people as they once were but as they might be. People who grow old can also grow love."

THOSE
WHO LOVE TO BE RIGHT
HATE TO BE WRONG

*T*he husband came into the house, brushing a late frost from the shoulders of his shirt. He offered to guide Jacob back to the path.

As they moved down the trail and away from the house, the man began to speak without turning to look at Jacob.

From the tone in the man's voice, Jacob knew the man was not seeking an answer but was like someone who, though blind, would move from room to room feeling the furniture, convincing himself that what he could not see was still in its place.

"My wife is very different now from the person I fell in love with," said the husband.

"Falling in love," said Jacob, "is very different than landing."

"But once my wife and I were a strength to each other. Now I don't know what holds us together," said the husband.

"Many of us spend our lives married to our weaknesses," said Jacob.

"Why get married, then?" asked the husband.

"Because," said Jacob, "a relationship is not a way for us to exhibit our strengths but to find our balance."

WHO IN OUR LIVES
ARE THE FLOWERS
WE SEE AS WEEDS?

*A*s Jacob began his descent from the mountains, he looked down and could see a village much like his own clinging to a corner of the valley beneath him. The village looked so much like his own, Jacob shut his eyes, opened them, and shut them again.

Jacob wondered for a moment if it was possible that he had somehow lost his way and returned home.

Without warning, a gust of wind, mixed with memory and rushing up the hill, caused Jacob's shirt to billow. Then, just as quickly, the wind died, and Jacob's shirt fell flat against his chest, leaving him alone with his memory—leaving him to wander down this distant hill into a distant valley.

Jacob moved down the path, which turned back and forth on itself toward the village. A narrow river twisted through the community, a river that seemed to bend like a finger, wiggling, hoping to draw Jacob close. When he arrived at the bank of the river, he sat to eat the last of his bread.

An old man lost in his thoughts walked next to the water. Noticing Jacob, he came over and sat next to him.

"I hope I am not bothering you," said the man.

Jacob pointed to the small yellow blossoms poking their heads from between the rocks. "Who in our lives," said Jacob, "are the flowers we see as weeds?"

Then Jacob offered the man half the bread that was left. The man looked at Jacob, not sure what to make of him. "You are a poor traveler. If I take your food, the sooner you will be hungry."

"To the poor," said Jacob, "the next meal is always an act of faith."

I AM SENDING AN ANGEL
IN FRONT OF YOU
TO GUARD YOU AS YOU GO
AND TO GUIDE YOU
TO THE PLACE I HAVE PREPARED

*T*he sky grew red and then began to pale to dusk. Jacob and the old man sat together shoulder to shoulder. Their manner with each other was not like men who had just met but as men who were being introduced to a friendship that had long existed but which they were just now discovering. In this way, Jacob met Joseph.

"What work do you?" asked Joseph.

"I am a baker," said Jacob.

Joseph laughed. "I used to be baker," he said, intrigued by the parallel. "But now I am afraid I am getting too old for my work."

"It is written that 'although we are not excused from the work, neither are we expected to finish it' " said Jacob.

"Yes," said Joseph, "but what will I do with my time?"

"When we treat time as a limit," said Jacob, "then time becomes a wall, a barrier we will die climbing. If we see our days as a river," Jacob motioned to the waters in front of them, "then we know time as a vehicle and realize we have all been born as passengers."

"Passengers on a difficult journey," said Joseph.

"Perhaps," said Jacob. "But think about the story of Noah. Even in the flood of death, it is the flood that supports the ark of life."

"And is that the lesson of Noah?" asked Joseph.

When Jacob began to speak again, his words came slowly, like a man stepping carefully from stone to stone in a distant garden.

"The lesson of Noah teaches us that there comes a time in each of our lives when it is necessary to build an ark, to create a structure in which we can hide—a habit or a place or an attitude within ourselves that will shelter us—if we are to survive life's terrible storms."

"Yes," said Joseph, interrupting, thinking back on the story he read as a child, "but why was Noah told to put a window in the ark? What could he see by doing this but the sadness of his fate?"

"My friend," said Jacob, "faith sees *beyond* fate. Noah was told to put a window in the ark so he could tell when the rain had stopped, and so we can remind others who have struggled to survive that they, too, should put a window in their ark, so all of us will know when it is time to come out from behind the habit of walls we build to survive."

"And what will we see then?" asked Joseph.

"We will see," said Jacob, "that the world is not always filled with a flood."

Joseph listened with his eyes while Jacob spoke; then, with a tone more plea than invitation, he asked, "Jacob, perhaps if you stay with me awhile you will turn my home into an ark."

"If two people accept each other's weaknesses," said Jacob, "then their vulnerability is an ark for both of them."

WHEN WE HAVE LOST
OUR WAY
IT IS NOT THE WAY
THAT IS LOST

*A*lthough Joseph had offered him his bed, Jacob folded his blankets in the front room, near the window. When Jacob woke, the morning star that had guided him so often to the bakery was still climbing in the window's corner pane.

A small mouse raced across the floor to its door in the molding. Sensing Jacob, the mouse stopped, lifted its head, and looked at him. "Hurry to your home," said Jacob. "I am the stranger."

Jacob prepared tea and sat quietly, allowing his patience to center himself. The cup warmed Jacob's hands. His eyes followed its rim, stared at its course, and saw in its endless truth that life is a race that could be run but never won.

When his cup was empty, Jacob could see where the potter's hand had begun the form. He could sense the momentum of the potter's wheel going round and round. He could watch himself, like the walls of the cup, rising not by his own effort to be more but as The Potter's hand held the clay to its own center.

Jacob bent his head, wrapped himself in his prayer shawl, and thanked God for taking the time to have tea with him on this morning.

WHEN WE DO NOT ACHIEVE
OUR EXPECTATIONS
WE USUALLY REWARD
OURSELVES
WITH DESPAIR

*B*y midmorning, Joseph's neighbors in the tiny community came to his house, using conversation as a way to mask their curiosity about the man he had brought home.

"Oh, Joseph," said a couple, the wife waving her hand in disgust, "our children are not growing up to be who we want them to be."

"Well . . ." said Joseph, not sure what to say. Then he turned to Jacob. The faces of the neighbors followed. *Well?* all three seemed to be asking.

Jacob saw himself where he had seen himself before, and he saw the faces of the neighbors and Joseph and their "Well?" hanging in the air.

"Well," said Jacob, answering his door out of instinct, "although it is natural that we worry about how our children will grow, we must remember that planting the seed does not make us the tree."

Unsure on the inside, the mother and father pushed their anger to the outside. "But, but . . . we had such hopes for our children."

Jacob, gesturing to calm the parents, began to move his hands as if he were patting down the soil around the base of a young plant.

"Like life itself," said Jacob, "your children are a gift to you, and only expectation can find disappointment in gifts that have not yet been opened."

CHANGE

....

IS THE ONLY CONSTANT

*L*ate that night, stories of what the parents had asked and what Joseph's guest had answered were whispered from door to door. Rumors ran like the river that flowed through the village. Tales were told about the stranger named Jacob.

Soon, people began to arrive at Joseph's home. They came alone at first, then two by two; they waited in line, hoping Jacob might ease their storm or calm a question that had broken over their lives.

"Jacob," said a young woman, "what does the future hold for me?"

"The future holds, but the present gives. Being where you are is the best way to get to where you are going," said Jacob.

"Jacob," said a student, his voice rising while he spoke, "the poet says, 'All the world can be seen in a single blade of grass.' What do you say?"

"Yes," said Jacob, "the world *can* be seen in a single blade of grass . . . but you must take the time to look."

"And what about life, tell us about life," shouted another voice, shoving the voices next to it aside.

"When we are young, we wonder what we will be," said Jacob. "When we are old we wonder what people will say of what we have become. When we face death we wonder where we are going."

"So, are you saying life is wonderful?" asked the voice, laughing at its own cleverness.

"No," said Jacob, returning the smile, "life is not always wonderful, but it is an experience filled with wonder."

DOING
IS THE WAY
WE USE ACTION
TO HIDE THE CHARACTER
WE ARE BEING

A young man anxious to make his point stood snapping his fingers and turning his head from side to side.

"Look, Jacob," he said without waiting to see if he had Jacob's attention, "I'm not so much of a thinker. I like to do things. I want to be somebody."

"*Doing* is the way we use action to hide the character we are being," said Jacob, his voice less clever than caring.

"That may be true for some people," said the young man, "but to me life is magic! I need action."

"All of us *are* magicians," said Jacob. "With great skill we shift who we are as if we were peas under walnut shells. Soon, we ourselves have no idea where we are hidden. Soon, pride in our camouflage causes us to become caught in our own sleight of hand."

"Weil," said the young man, "at least I'm not old like my grandfather. He sits with his chin resting on his cane, doing nothing for hours. I have my whole life in front of me."

"You do have your life in front of you," said Jacob, "and yet life is an experience not only of breadth but of depth. As you grow older, the game of life goes inside, makes room for memory. This interior life is no less real, and in some ways is more private, more yours."

"But," said the young man, "what do you think my grandfather spends so much time thinking about?"

"Maybe he is thinking about you," said Jacob.

"About me?"

"Yes," said Jacob, "maybe he's worried that his grandson is living only on the surface of life, and he wonders when you'll come inside."

TRUST YOURSELF
BY TRUSTING
THERE IS SOMETHING
GREATER THAN YOURSELF

A woman in her middle years kept allowing others to go before her. At last she took a deep breath, summoning her courage to step forward.

"Jacob," said the woman, exhaling in shallow breaths as she began, "my husband died recently and I'm not sure I want to go on living."

"Be patient with yourself," said Jacob. "When we lose someone we love, often our ability to love life is also lost for a while."

"Even though very few people knew my husband," said the woman as if she needed to explain her grief, "he was my best friend."

"Anyone who has suffered a loss," said Jacob, "knows that a man does not have to be a hero for his death to be a tragedy."

WE ARE THE PAINTER,
THE PAINT,
AND THE PAINTING

Jacob introduced silence to the conversation, offering the woman across from him the quiet to share her sorrow.

The woman held at the hem of the silence as if it were a blanket.

"It's just that since my husband's passed away, I feel so alone," she said.

"We are all alone," said Jacob, "only before, you and your husband were alone together."

The woman sighed.

"Let me tell you a story," said Jacob.

"Once there was a woman who lay in bed trying to understand her life. Eventually, she fell asleep and into a deep dream. In her dream, the woman saw herself as a child, saw herself staring from a window in her parents' house, saw herself looking out at the world as a great mysterious painting, a painting without end, a confusion within her vision but not yet her understanding.

"Turning in her sleep, the child became a woman. Now, she saw herself beginning to know her world, saw mystery give way to understanding, saw she could identify the figures in her painting . . . including herself, wondered why it had taken her so long to know what she really knew.

"Still the dream continued, and soon the woman experienced herself growing older with no more forecast than anything else she had come to know. Now, she saw that the people and landmarks by which she understood and guided her life were being pulled from her painting. Her painting had become a puzzle, and the pieces of her life were disappearing. What she knew could no longer be counted on to hold its place.

"Even her own continent, she saw, was becoming an island. Without having cast off, she found she was floating out to sea. She found she was leaving not because she had left but because the world that had always surrounded and defined her, the world she had always known . . . had left *her*.

"The territory of trust upon which her life was constructed was now threatened. Soon, she feared, her own piece of the puzzle would be removed. But in some ways she knew it didn't matter. Because in some ways she knew she was already gone. Gone but not absent. And when she saw even her fear sweep past her, a peace she had never experienced came over the woman."

"And then?" asked the woman across from Jacob, absorbed in the story.

"And then," said Jacob, "the woman woke and discovered that she had been asleep."

"Jacob, are you telling me not to worry because life is only a dream?"

"No," said Jacob. "I am telling you only that worrying is not the way to dream."

WHAT WE SEE IN OTHERS
IS ANOTHER WAY
OF LOOKING AT OURSELVES

Among those who stood at the edge of the conversations and listened to Jacob was a young woman with child. When Jacob's eyes met hers, she found herself asking a question.

"I'm about to give birth, Jacob," she said. "What can you tell me?"

"The birth of innocence is the door to experience," said Jacob.

"And experience?"

"Ah," said Jacob. "Experience is a mask we wear to hide our innocence."

"Maybe you are right, Jacob," said the young woman. "It's just that I see so much more strength in others than I see in myself."

"That is your innocence," said Jacob. "Experience will teach you that what we see in others is another way of looking at ourselves."

WHEREVER WE STOP
ON OUR JOURNEY
THE FIRST PERSON
WE WILL MEET
IS OURSELF

When those who had waited to see Jacob returned to their homes, Joseph shut the door slowly.

Jacob remained behind the low table where he had sat throughout the day, his elbow resting on the table, and the side of his head cradled in the curve of his hand.

Although there were three stars in the sky, the moon had not yet climbed above the hills that circled the village. Reciting an ancient prayer, Joseph lit two white candles. The light danced on the wax, made the two men's shadows into mountains, and cast the mountains against the wall so they appeared to rest on Jacob's shoulders.

Joseph lifted the bread for their evening meal and then put it down without uttering the blessing. Joseph looked at his friend and then spoke with apology.

"I'm sorry, Jacob. When I invited you into my home, I did not know so many others would come to see you."

Jacob looked at Joseph and thought of his friend Samuel chasing the pigeons from the back of the bakery.

"Jacob," asked Joseph, "do you *mind* those who come to see you?"

"It is my own blindness that surrounds me," said Jacob. "Wherever a man stops on his journey, the first person he meets is himself."

Again Joseph lifted the bread and again he returned it to the table.

"Does that mean we are forever limited to what we already know?" asked Joseph.

The shadows on the walls behind Jacob moved lower, making him part of their profile.

"When we are born," said Jacob, "it is like being admitted to a large room for the first time. In this space, the lights are diminished so our eyes may focus on the stage and the play that is occurring. Unfortunately, over time we become so involved in the play that we forget we are sitting in the dark."

"But we do share a common vision, don't we?"

"And a common blindness," said Jacob.

"What do you mean?" asked Joseph.

"Often in life we choose to be distracted rather than disturbed," said Jacob, "but vision is more than an agreed-upon blindness. It is more than measuring the rut we live in and saying it is not a rut because we all arrive at the same measurements."

"People don't want to hear this," said Joseph with a tone of warning.

"You are right," said Jacob. "We make the day dark by shutting our eyes. When we have put out our candles so we can go to sleep, we don't want to be disturbed."

"Then how do we avoid these traps?" asked Joseph.

"By remembering that the truth will not set us free if we honestly want to be slaves," said Jacob.

Joseph lifted the bread to say the blessing and looked across the table at his friend. "Jacob," said Joseph, "thank you for being here."

"It is in *God's* mercy that He brought us out of Egypt," said Jacob, "and in His mercy for *me* that He has brought us together."

WISDOM
BELONGS TO THOSE
WHO CAN GRASP IT

*T*hat night while Jacob slept, he dreamed he was again at home.

He heard the wind playing its flute while he walked in the low grass next to the river. He saw his pants still dusted with flour from the bakery. He watched the children chasing one another after school and listened while they told stories that once he had told them.

Stay on the river long enough, thought Jacob, and everything on the shore will float past you.

A tapping, like soft rain on a wood roof, began at the door and woke Jacob from his dream. He sat up in bed and stepped out of his blankets.

Through the window, a half-moon, as hidden as it was bright, stood straight up, radiant in its ring of fog.

Jacob opened the door. There, facing him across the memory of time and distance, was the old man to whom he had once offered the warmth of the bakery on a winter morning. Now, however, the visitor was no longer dressed in rags.

"May I come in?" asked the voice.

Jacob held the door open, watching the moment move forward.

As the visitor entered, Joseph woke and came out of his room. When he saw the old man, Joseph seemed to shrink with deference. The old man, however, did not take his eyes from Jacob.

"Jacob," said Joseph, stuttering, "this . . . this is the Elder from the Council of Sages."

Joseph rushed to get a chair, which he placed behind the old man. The Elder sat wearily, and Joseph backed into a corner, almost disappearing in the shadows, unsure what to do next.

Now Jacob and the Elder remained alone in the center of the room, their figures bathed in the moon and the silence.

"When we first met," said the old man, scratching at the stillness, "I had sought you out, though I did not want you to know who I was."

"We *are* nothing," said Jacob, "and we become something more only by knowing this."

"Maybe you are right," said the old man, nodding his head in affirmation. "However, soon I will be *less* than nothing, and there are none in the Council prepared to come after me." His voice slipped the bounds of the room.

"Be patient," said Jacob. "Patience is also preparation. It is the action before the act. Wisdom arrives when we are willing to journey to our ignorance."

"But now," said the Elder, his tone beginning to reveal the strength of hidden intention, "now that you have journeyed to us, my wish is for you to head the Council of Sages when I am gone."

Jacob could hear Joseph gasp from the shadows.

"Thank you, but I am a baker," said Jacob, answering as if the Elder's request were simply a case of mistaken identity.

"Where?" said the old man, stretching the word forever.

And Jacob did not know what to answer.

"Where if not here?" said the old man.

And Jacob did not know what to answer.

"Give us the bread of your wisdom," said the Elder, with insistence.

"The wisdom is not mine," said Jacob. "We cannot suspect in others what we do not know in ourselves."

"Perhaps, then, in time you will decide to stay with us?"

"Perhaps," said Jacob, without promise. "Waiting is also a season of growth."

"Then I will wait," said the Elder. "Like David, whose determination could find innocence in the hills of experience, I will be your shepherd."

"But I am not a sheep," said Jacob, "and you cannot find what is not lost."

The old man took Jacob's hand. Jacob could feel the dry flesh, like aged parchment, cupped and held against his own.

"I told you I would not forget you, Jacob," said the Elder, smiling.

When Jacob answered, his voice was filled with memory. "The people and places in our life are like a dream. Too often we forget this until we wake and they are gone."

THE MEANING OF LIFE
....
CAN BE FOUND
....
ONLY IN THE EXPERIENCE
....
OF LIVING

*T*he next morning, when Joseph came in to stir the fire against the cold, he could see the people already gathering in front of his house with the hope of meeting Jacob.

"Jacob," asked Joseph, his curiosity like an itch that demanded to be scratched, "how did you sleep?"

Jacob looked up from a small prayer book he had borrowed from the shelves behind him. He said nothing.

"Jacob, does it upset you that the Elder hid his identity when you first met?"

"No," said Jacob. "Most of us wear masks not so we won't be seen but so we won't be recognized."

"The Elder must see great things in you, Jacob," said Joseph.

"Vision," said Jacob, "is seeing where we are *not* looking."

"Some of the people say you may be a prophet," said Joseph, raising his eyebrows and watching Jacob closely.

Jacob shook his head from side to side. "The conviction of ignorance is an argument blindly following what it does not know."

"But it is true, isn't it, that the Elder wants you to take his place?" asked Joseph, with the tentativeness of a man who already had an answer for what he was asking.

"Though it is possible," said Jacob, "for someone to find himself captain of a ship he never intended to sail, I am a baker, and as important as it is to think about who you could be, it is no less important to remember who you are."

TELLING THE TRUTH
THE WAY WE WANT
TO HEAR IT
IS OFTEN THE WAY
WE LIE TO OURSELVES

*T*he days grew shorter, but the line outside Joseph's home did not diminish. People now simply added Jacob's name to the list they took to the marketplace.

One middle-aged man, determined that no one would go in before him, glared at the others and dared Jacob to answer his questions.

"Because I have lied about another person, the people in the village have called me a thief. Should I be punished in the same way?"

"No," said Jacob, almost with disinterest.

"That's what I told them," said the man, jerking his thumb at the crowd behind him.

"Your punishment should be *greater*," said Jacob, taking the man by surprise.

The man sputtered curses, but Jacob continued. "You see, a thief may be forced to return what he has stolen, but when you tell a lie, those around you cannot be forced to return what they have heard anymore than a man can give away what he has seen."

"But, I didn't lie to *everyone*."

"In the seed of a lie," said Jacob, "is a forest of deceit. This forest shadows even those who did not hear the lie."

THE CHALLENGE IS NOT TO
DIE HEROICALLY
BUT TO LIVE BRAVELY

A young couple came forward together. The girl's hands clutched at the sides of her long skirt. The boy pulled without awareness at strands of his hair. Finally, they stepped across the doorway.

"Jacob," said the girl, her emotions bursting, "life doesn't make sense."

"Well," said Jacob, "perhaps that is because you were not born from the mind of your mother."

"But we are no longer children, Jacob. And though we're about to be married, we're both nervous because we're afraid."

"Good," said Jacob.

"Good?" said the couple in unison, incredulous.

"Yes," said Jacob. "Only those who are afraid to fear, fear too much. Strength is not the absence of weakness but how we wrestle *with* our weaknesses."

WE
ARE GOD'S FINGERPRINTS

A man, stiff in his proudness, looked down at Jacob.

"Jacob, I want my life to make an impression on others."

"Every life *is* an impression," said Jacob.

"What do you mean?" asked the man.

And Jacob answered, "We are God's fingerprints."

THOSE
WHO HAVE EVERYTHING
DREAM
OF NEW APPETITES

Jacob placed both hands flat on the low table before him and pushed himself up. His knees were stiff. He decided to take a walk by the river.

While Jacob walked, a group of children playing ran past him, waved hello, and then, concerned, asked him if he thought it would rain.

"Don't worry," said Jacob.

"How do you know it won't rain?" asked the children.

"I don't," said Jacob. "I know only that the sunshine uses rain to make rainbows."

Jacob walked on until he found the inlet where he and Joseph had first met.

Standing by the water's edge, Jacob saw a man angrily throwing stones into the river.

"Hey, Jacob!" shouted the man. "Let me ask you a question." He did not wait for Jacob's answer.

"Why do people treat a man as rich as me like a dog?"

"Perhaps," said Jacob, "it is because *only* a dog will bury his bone rather than share it."

The man snarled at Jacob's answer. "What the others say makes me angry. I'm trying to decide what I should do."

"Well," said Jacob, "it sounds as if your only confusion is in trying to decide what to be angry about next."

"And what do you think I should do?" asked the man.

"The only decision you have to make," answered Jacob, "is whether you are trying to find your way or lose your temper."

FAITH
PARTS THE SEA;
A FOOL
PUSHES THE RIVER

*R*emembering times as a boy, Jacob bent by the river and dropped a flotilla of small sticks and leaves into the water's flow. He watched his boats race and tumble around one bend only to be caught in another. In this rush and pause and rush again, Jacob saw the pulse of nature's pace.

"You see," said a woman who came up behind Jacob, "clearly we are not in control of where our lives are going."

"Perhaps," said Jacob, turning toward the voice, "but we are nevertheless responsible for how we conduct ourselves as we are carried on."

"What about when we die?" asked the woman.

"When we are young, death is a rumor. When we are old, death is a door," said Jacob.

"But not knowing what's on the other side of the door is frightening," said the woman, pushing Jacob with her anxiety.

"Why?" asked Jacob. "Before you were born you were on the other side of the door and do you remember being frightened then?"

"Well, what about when we lose our parents?" asked the woman.

Jacob answered with calm. "When we are born, it is out of a great darkness that we find our parents. When our parents are gone they can no more be lost to us than we can lose ourselves."

"But surely," asked the woman, turning to enjoy the wit of her question, "there must be some way for us to lose ourselves."

"Only when we place too much importance on who we are do we misplace our self," said Jacob.

IT IS NOT
THAT LIFE IS A JUNGLE,
BUT THAT THE JUNGLE
IS PART OF LIFE

A man running to his own rush attached himself to Jacob as he was returning through the
fields to Joseph's home.

"Jacob," said the man, motioning to the world
around him, "I have made it my life's work to
save the trees and the rivers. Is this enough?"

"Save the moments also," said Jacob.

"Will that make my work more important?"
asked the man.

"It will make your life more," said Jacob. "If
we do not find our moments, we lose our way."

"Yes, but what about the tragedy in nature?" said the man, his manner intensifying. "What else should I be doing?"

"Often in life," said Jacob, "the solution to our problems comes not so much from what we *start* doing but from what we *stop* doing."

"Then things will soon be better?" asked the man.

"Things will be different," said Jacob.

"How can you be sure of this?"

"Because in the nature of things," said Jacob, "the seasons change."

THOSE
WHO DO NOT BEND,
BREAK

*B*efore the sun had climbed its ladder the next morning, a couple stood waiting to see Jacob. Their hands were knotted and hard and looked like the land where they labored.

"Jacob," said the man and woman, clearly uncomfortable with being public about what they felt, "there has been much sadness in our lives."

"Tragedy is part of the landscape," said Jacob softly.

"Yes," said the woman, almost shuddering at speaking so openly, "and we have been standing in the rain."

When Jacob answered the woman, his voice was more concerned with caring than with being correct. "In each of our lives," said Jacob, "there comes a time when we will stand in the rain and feel that God is crying for us."

"Tell me, Jacob," said the man, "is this just as true for the strong as it is for the weak?"

"In life," said Jacob, "those who do not bend, break."

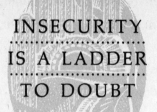

INSECURITY
IS A LADDER
TO DOUBT

A man filled with the energy of his plans moved back and forth from one foot to the other until he could finally push forward and gather Jacob's attention.

"Listen, Jacob, I'm going to do great things with my life. And what I want to know is, how does it feel to be so well known?"

"The question is not if we are well known but if we know ourselves well," said Jacob. "Our status among others is not a burden, it is an illusion. Vanity is its own mirror, a way we are seduced by what we *want* to see."

"But I *want* to feel like somebody important," said the man.

Jacob smiled and then spoke. "What is important is that you like the somebody you are."

BECAUSE WE LIVE WITH QUESTIONS DOES NOT MEAN WE DIE WITH ANSWERS

A girl who wanted to see Jacob drew circle after circle with the toe of her shoe while she waited. Although she had passed Joseph's house many times, she had never spoken to Jacob directly. Now, as the numbers around her diminished, the void pulled her forward.

"Jacob," she began, still looking at her feet, "what have you learned from talking with so many people?"

Jacob said nothing.

"Aren't you going to answer me?" asked the girl, lifting her head to see if she had Jacob's attention.

Still, Jacob said nothing.

"Why aren't you going to answer me?" asked the girl.

"Because," said Jacob, "silence cannot be argued."

The girl laughed and then her voice swelled with earnestness. "Jacob, I'm thinking of becoming a teacher."

"Teaching is the highest charity of wisdom," said Jacob.

"But what if I fail to achieve wisdom?" asked the girl.

"Life is not a failure because we die but only if we fail to live," said Jacob.

"Then, will I be wise when I am old?" asked the girl.

Jacob brushed back the girl's hair that had fallen across her face. "Because we live with questions does not mean we die with answers."

FINDING OUR WAY
IS NOT THE SAME
AS FINDING THE STRENGTH
TO CARRY ON

A young man, beaming with good intentions, presented himself to Jacob and announced, "One day I hope to be as wise as you."

Jacob thought back through his own life. "When we are young," he said, "we seek the wisdom to find our way. As we grow older, what we pray for is strength."

"The strength to do what?"

"To carry on," answered Jacob.

"And does God give us that strength through prayer?" asked the young man, his voice hemmed with hope.

"Prayer begins not so much with God's hand reaching toward ours," answered Jacob, "but with *our* hand stretching toward God's."

"But what about heaven, Jacob?" said the young man, his voice pushing for an answer it could pocket. "How can we find our way to heaven?"

"We find our way to heaven," said Jacob, "by caring about those who live on earth."

"And if we don't care," asked the young man, "what then?"

"God does not threaten us," said Jacob, "except with the lack of compassion we show others."

REALITY
IS ONLY A MEMORY
AHEAD OF ITS TIME

*A*t the end of the line, at the end of the day, waiting at the edge of her patience, was an old woman. When she spoke, her voice was neither pressing nor rushed and yet shrill with its own urgency.

"I am old, Jacob, and you are not so young."

Jacob laughed and looked up from his weariness. "Age is not the mark of time but how we mark our time. Living is the best preparation for dying."

The woman waved off Jacob's remarks, not disagreeing but using her years as an allowance to be almost rude. "Those who I have known are all gone. I feel like I am also dead."

"The dead are not gone, but we are all going," said Jacob.

"Where are we going?" asked the old woman, turning her palms upward as if prepared to receive directions.

"I'm glad you asked," said Jacob, "because that is a question for the living."

"But, Jacob," asked the woman, her voice pulled tight, "in reality what is the answer?"

"Reality," said Jacob, "is only a memory ahead of its time."

SOMETIMES
WE MUST LEAVE OUR HOUSE
IN ORDER TO COME HOME

*T*he day was done. As the last person left, Jacob raised his shoulders and tried to give ease to his back. He thought of how Max would put his shoulder to the sacks of flour and slide them effortlessly across the floor of the bakery. Jacob could feel his own shoulder against the load that others had balanced on him and felt, even in this way, still a baker.

Joseph came over and offered Jacob a cup of tea.

Jacob accepted the tea and then set the cup down. He began, without explanation, to wrap his prayer shawl, putting his few possessions in his worn canvas bag.

"Where are you going?" asked Joseph, his voice uncertain to see his friend packing, unsure what to say.

"I am going home," said Jacob.

"To do what?" asked Joseph.

"To be a baker."

"And the Council of Sages?" asked Joseph in awe and disbelief.

"Do they need a baker?" asked Jacob.

"They need you to be their *tzadik*, their holy man."

"The Council's work is to be wise. My work is to bake bread."

"But you will see," said Joseph, "soon it will be like here. It will be impossible for you to get any work done."

"It will be possible," said a voice from the doorway, with quiet reassurance.

Before Jacob could turn his head, he knew it was his friend Samuel. Before Jacob could smile, Samuel moved forward and embraced him.

"Even in our tiny village," said Samuel, "we heard about Jacob the baker and where you were living and all the people who waited to talk with you."

Jacob, shifting the focus from himself, introduced Joseph to Samuel. The two men shook hands, meeting themselves in each other.

Then Samuel rushed ahead, anxious as always to tell his story. "Jacob, all of us at home have been thinking about the things you taught us. What we realized is that we want you to come back and be Jacob the baker."

Now Jacob, like Noah, looked up through the window, through the roof in his ark, saw the sky clearing, knew the flood was retreating.

Samuel placed his hands on Jacob's shoulders and held him at arm's length. "So? Will you do it, will you come home?"

And while Jacob said nothing, the tears that ran down his cheeks were already finding the path to his heart.

"But, Jacob, if you go, what shall I do?" asked Joseph.

"You?" asked Jacob, smiling. "You should be my friend."

"Then, I will miss you," said Joseph.

"A friend is someone who allows you distance, but is *never* far away," said Jacob.

"And what of those who *are* far away?" asked Joseph. "What of those who do not live in the community where Jacob the baker lives? Who will answer their questions?"

"A wise man is not fooled by answers," said Jacob, "and a fool is not wise for having them.

"Strength of character is not measured by who we support but by knowing we all lean on one another.

"Those who are looking for Jacob the baker will find their way inside themselves."

About the Author

Noah benShea is a poet, philosopher, and teacher. His work has been praised by theologians and scholars while his timeless tales of Jacob the Baker are now told and retold not only in North America but around the world. Born in Toronto, Noah benShea lives with his wife and two children in Santa Barbara, California, where he is also one of the owners and president of a national bread company.